Francis Poulenc

Three Novelettes
for piano

Revised edition, 1999
Edited by Millan Sachania
with an Introduction by Caroline Potter

Chester Music

POULENC
Three Novelettes

INTRODUCTION

Poulenc first made an impact on the Parisian musical scene as early as 1918, when the 19-year-old composer's *Rapsodie nègre* was first performed. Although his career stretched over four decades, his musical style changed little. The three *Novelettes* perfectly illustrate the essential unity of his style : while the first two pieces were written in 1927 and 1928, and originally published together, the third was not composed until 1959. Though there are no thematic or other precise musical links between the pieces, they form a well-contrasted and stylistically consistent set.

The dedicatee of the first *Novelette*, in C major, was an elderly lady who was a friend of the Poulenc family. The composer had stayed in Virginie Liénard's home in Nazelles on several occasions since 1923 ; the closeness of their relationship is illustrated by the fact that he called her 'Tante Liénard'. The piece was finished at her home in October 1927, and Poulenc later dedicated his piano suite *Les soirées de Nazelles* (1930–36) to her memory. The second *Novelette*, in B flat, is dedicated to the music critic Louis Laloy, a friend and supporter of Poulenc's from the beginning of his composing career. This piece was finished in 1928, and the American scholar Keith Daniel sees a musical connection between this piece and the third of Poulenc's rumbustious *Chansons gaillardes*, composed in the same period.

The much later third *Novelette* was commissioned for the Chester *Centenary Album* (1960), and is dedicated to 'my dear friend Gibson'—R. Douglas Gibson, then the director of J. & W. Chester. There is a further Chester connection, too, as the piece is based on a theme from Manuel de Falla's *El amor brujo*, which was composed in 1916 and published by the same firm. Falla and Poulenc met in 1918 at the home of Poulenc's Spanish piano teacher, Ricardo Viñes, the great virtuoso and the dedicatee of many of Ravel's piano works. The close friendship between the two composers lasted until Falla's departure from Spain for Argentina in 1939 in the aftermath of the Spanish Civil War. He was the dedicatee of Poulenc's Trio for oboe, bassoon and piano, a work to which the composers referred as 'our piece' in their correspondence. In a letter to Falla dated 29 January 1923, Poulenc told him that 'I ADORE' *El amor brujo*, and he asked whether Chester might send him a score.

The theme used by Poulenc comes from the 'Pantomime' movement of *El amor brujo* ; Falla himself must have been fond of the theme, as he reworked it in his *Homenaje 'Le Tombeau de Claude Debussy'* (1920), composed for guitar for an issue of the *Revue musicale* dedicated to Debussy's memory. Poulenc simplifies the theme, changing its unusual 7/8 metre in order to fit the idea into a more conventional 3/8. The theme is heard four times, and, unusually for Poulenc, there is no contrasting section.

In an interview with Claude Rostand in 1954, Poulenc said that he often found interpretations of his piano music disappointing, though his advice to performers was nothing if not blunt. 'I hate rubato', he stated ; 'never prolong or shorten a note value'. He added that 'people *never* use enough pedal'. His fondness for a blurred piano sound doubtless stemmed from Viñes, an acknowledged master of pedalling, and Poulenc's favourite metaphor for pedalling was 'put butter in the sauce'! He stressed that arpeggio or repeated-note figurations should be played with plenty of pedal, and that the melody should sing above this blurred background (the opening of the third *Novelette* is a good illustration of this).

Poulenc is best known for his important contributions to the *mélodie* and for his choral music ; his piano music is more uneven in quality, and only the *Trois mouvements perpétuels* (1919) are frequently performed. But the *Trois novelettes* are typical of their composer's charm-with-a-twist and illustrative of his accessible yet multi-layered piano writing.

Caroline Potter

EDITORIAL PREFACE

In preparing this new edition of Poulenc's *Novelettes*, I have taken the opportunity not only to remedy the various notational inaccuracies and the juxtaposition of engraving styles which characterised the previous edition, but also to revisit and re-evaluate the source materials. The resulting score compromises between taking a strictly scholarly line and supplying an edition of practical value to the performing musician.

In terms of the source materials, *Novelette* No. 3 presents the fewest problems to the editor. There are two available sources : the composer's manuscript and the first published edition (1960). This new edition takes the autograph manuscript as its source.

Three sources were available for *Novelette* No. 2 : a copyist's manuscript (1929?) ; the first printed edition (1930), prepared from the copyist's manuscript ; and the revised edition (1939). The autograph manuscript was unavailable for consultation. This new edition thus follows the copyist's score but incorporates the 1939 amendments (see below).

The first *Novelette* has the most complicated source history of the three. There are two autograph manuscripts. The present location of one of these (which is apparently undated) is unknown, and accordingly it has had no input into this new edition. The other, dated 1928, is deposited at Yale University and was presented by Poulenc to Vladimir Horowitz. There is also a copyist's manuscript (1929?), which includes corrections in Poulenc's hand. This source differs in many of its performance directions and articulations from those found in the 'Horowitz' autograph. The copyist's score gave rise to the first edition (1930). As with the second, the first *Novelette* was revised in 1939. The alterations, though, amounted only to the addition of initial metronome markings, the enharmonic re-spelling of a few notes, some changes in the stem directions, and the insertion of some cautionary accidentals and a few ties and slurs. The present edition takes the copyist's score as the primary source but incorporates the 1939 revisions and some details found in the 'Horowitz' manuscript.

I have corrected patent omissions and errors in all three *Novelettes* and have inserted some cautionary accidentals to aid legibility. I have also aimed at rationalising Poulenc's notational practice, particularly with regard to beaming. Poulenc often disregards modern beaming conventions, breaking beams where they should not normally be fractured, or omitting them altogether—inscribing instead a series of quavers or semiquavers with individual flags. The notation of this edition conforms to modern-day practice where Poulenc's 'offending' style seems to be due primarily to habit or carelessness. In instances where the irregular beaming might stem from Poulenc's concern for clarifying the rhythmic units, I have retained his notation only where the musical groupings are not reinforced by means of, say, slurring or context. In contentious or doubtful contexts, however, Poulenc's notational method has been conserved. Finally, I have generally made the articulation and notational styles of parallel passages conform, though each instance has been subject to the verdict of my musical judgment.

Millan Sachania

Pour ma tante Liénard

NOVELETTE
IN C MAJOR

I

FRANCIS POULENC

4

Nazelles, octobre 1927

à Louis Laloy

NOVELETTE
IN B♭ MINOR

II

FRANCIS POULENC

Très rapide et rythmé ♩ = 138

Absolument sans ralentir

Amboise, 1928

To my dear friend Gibson

NOVELETTE

IN E MINOR

III

Sur un thème de Manuel de Falla

(*El Amor Brujo*)

Andantino tranquillo ♪ = 120

FRANCIS POULENC

baigné de pédales

Note: *The House of Chester, 1860–1960: Centenary Album* (Chester, 1960), for which this *Novelette* was specially written, provides a facsimile of the composer's manuscript.

© Copyright for all countries 1960, 1999
Chester Music Limited, 14–15 Berners Street, London W1T 3LJ

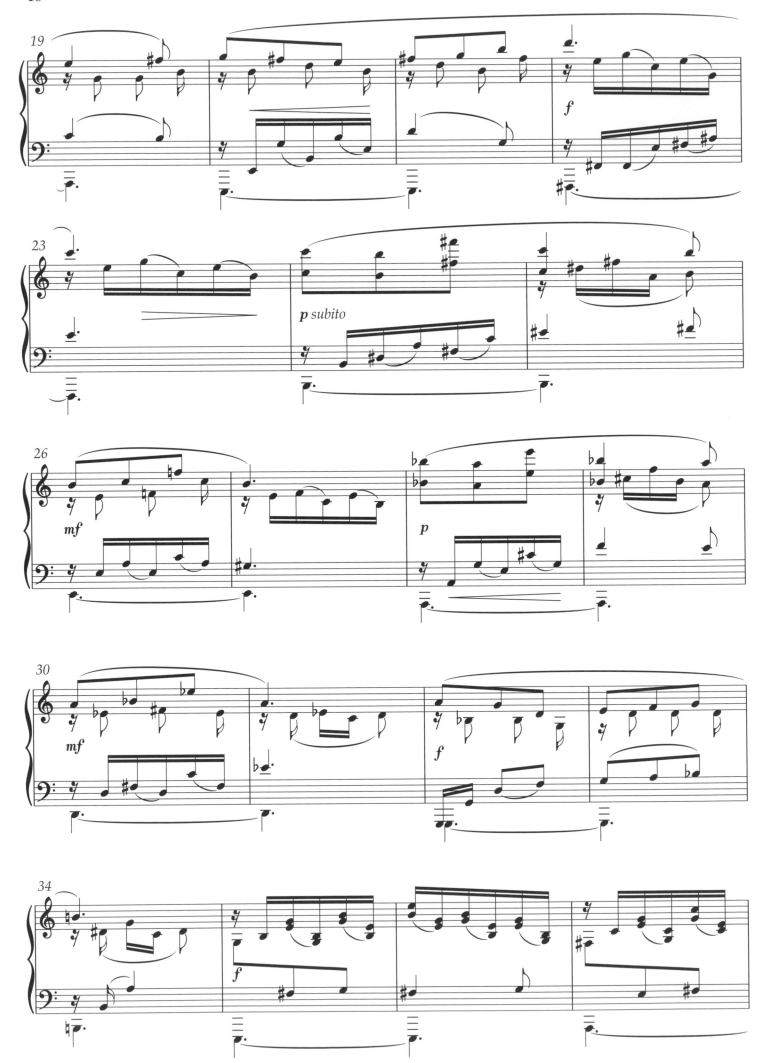

Brive, juin 1959